D1144707

ITALY

Clare Hibbert

WAYLAND

FACT CAT

Get your paws on this fantastic new mega-series from Wayland!

Join our Fact Cat on a journey of fun learning about every subject under the sun!

First published in 2014 by Wayland
© Wayland 2014

Wayland
Hachette Children's Books
338 Euston Road
London NW1 3BH

Wayland Australia
Level 17/207 Kent Street
Sydney NSW 2000

 Produced for Wayland by
White-Thomson Publishing Ltd
www.wtpub.co.uk
+44 (0) 843 208 7460

Editor: Clare Hibbert
Design: Rocket Design (East Anglia) Ltd
Fact Cat illustrations: Shutterstock/Julien Troneur
Other illustrations: Stefan Chabluk
Consultant: Kate Ruttle

A catalogue for this title is available from the British Library

ISBN: 978 0 7502 8214 7
ebook ISBN: 978 0 7502 8 8309
Dewey Number: 945-dc23
10 9 8 7 6 5 4 3 2 1

Wayland is a division of Hachette Children's Books,
an Hachette UK company.
www.hachette.co.uk

Printed and bound in China

Picture and illustration credits:
Chabluk, Stefan: 4; Dreamstime: Lsantilli 7, Travelpeter 8, Mario Madrona Barrera 15, Pasquale Bellomo 16, M Rohana 17, Valeria Cantone 19; Shutterstock: KKulikov cover, Anton_Ivanov 6, Marc Scott-Parkin 11, Serafino Mozzo 12; SuperStock: Marka 18; Thinkstock: danbreckwoldt/iStock 1, sborisov/iStock 5, rz_design/iStock 9, Medioimages/Photodisc 10, momokey/iStock 13, federicofoto/iStock 14, sborisov/iStock 22; TopFoto: The Granger Collection 21; Wikimedia: L Prang & Co, Boston/Library of Congress 20.

Every effort has been made to clear copyright.
Should there be any inadvertent omission,
please apply to the publisher for rectification.

The author, Clare Hibbert, is a writer and editor specialising in children's information books.

The consultant, Kate Ruttle, is a literacy expert and SENCO, and teaches in Suffolk.

FACT CAT FACT

There is a question for you

CONTENTS

WELCOME TO ITALY

Italy is a country in southern Europe. People think it is shaped like a high-heeled boot, sticking out into the Mediterranean Sea.

SWITZERLAND
LIECHTENSTEIN
AUSTRIA
Alps
Dolomites
SLOVENIA
CROATIA
Milan
Venice
Turin
ITALY
SAN MARINO
FRANCE
Apennines
Florence
Pisa
Siena
Elba
Corsica (France)
Rome
VATICAN CITY
Naples
Vesuvius
Capri
Sardinia
Stromboli
Mediterranean Sea
Sicily
Etna
ALGERIA
TUNISIA

Italy surrounds two of the world's smallest countries. Find out what their names are.

Italy → EUROPE

Rome is the **capital** city of Italy. It has many old buildings. Some are more than 2,000 years old and were built in **ancient Roman** times.

Ancient Romans visited an enormous **amphitheatre** called the Colosseum to watch **gladiators** fight.

FACT CAT FACT

The Colosseum had seats for around 50,000 **spectators**.

CITIES

Rome is Italy's biggest city. More than 2.6 million people live there. Milan is the next largest city. It is in the far north of the country.

Milan has a grand shopping **mall** that was built around 150 years ago. It is named after Vittorio Emanuele II. Who was he?

The Mole Antonelliana is one of Turin's main **landmarks**. It is a museum. It has a four-sided dome.

Naples and Turin are the third and fourth largest cities. Naples is a busy **port** on the west coast. Turin, in northwest Italy, has lots of car factories.

FACT CAT FACT

The Mole Antonelliana is a museum of cinema. It is 167.5 metres tall – the world's tallest museum!

THE LAND

Italy has two big **mountain ranges**. The Dolomites are in the far north. They are part of the Alps. The Apennines run down the eastern part of Italy from north to south.

Just south of the Alps are three large lakes. Find out their names.

Italy has **active volcanoes**. One of the most famous ones is Vesuvius, near Naples. It is famous for destroying the ancient Roman cities of Pompeii and Herculaneum when it erupted nearly 2,000 years ago.

Etna, on Sicily, is Europe's tallest active volcano. It stands around 3,330 metres tall. The craters at the top spit out **lava** and ash.

FACT CAT FACT

The volcano Stromboli is an island off the coast of Sicily. It has been erupting non-stop for more than 2,000 years.

ISLANDS

There are more than 70 islands in the sea around Italy. Sicily and Sardinia are the largest. Elba is the next in size.

Capri is just off the coast of Naples. One of its top tourist attractions is a **sea cave** filled with blue light. Can you find out its name?

The city of Venice in northeastern Italy is made up of more than a hundred tiny islands. They are separated by **canals** and connected by hundreds of bridges.

On special occasions, people in Venice take a **gondola**. They pay a **fare** to the gondolier.

FOOD

Italian pasta and pizza are famous all over the world. Pasta is made with wheat flour and water. It comes in more than 100 shapes and sizes, including shells and stars.

Pizza is a flat bread with toppings. It is baked in a very hot oven. Find out what goes on a margherita pizza.

The Italians love sweet things. Cannoli are pastries from Sicily. They have a sweet, creamy filling made with **ricotta cheese**. Ice cream is popular during the hot summer months.

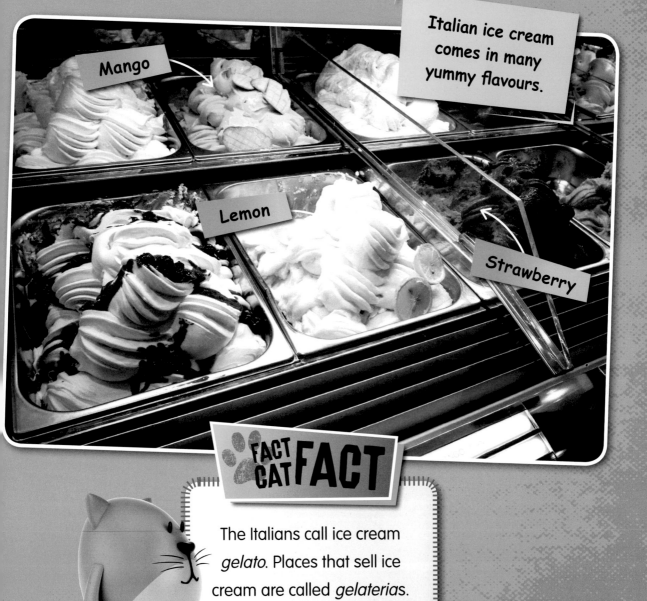

Italian ice cream comes in many yummy flavours.

Mango

Lemon

Strawberry

FACT CAT FACT

The Italians call ice cream *gelato*. Places that sell ice cream are called *gelateria*s.

WILDLIFE

Italy has more than 55,000 different types of animal. Some very **rare** kinds live in the Apennine Mountains. They include golden eagles, grey wolves and brown bears.

There are only a few brown bears left in Italy. They are called Marsican brown bears. Find out the name of the **national park** where they live.

Sardinia has wild sheep called mouflon living on its steep, wooded hillsides. They feed on scrubby grass and shrubs.

Both male and female mouflon have horns. The **rams** use their horns for bashing each other. It's their way of deciding which is the most important ram in the herd.

FACT CAT FACT

Italy is home to the world's smallest **mammal**. The tiny Etruscan shrew weighs less than a sugar lump!

FESTIVALS

The Venice **Carnival** takes place in spring. There are parties, **masked balls** and parades. People wear **historic** costumes and amazing masks.

At the end of the Venice Carnival, there is a prize for the most beautiful mask. Find out what masks can be made of.

At the Palio, the horses do three laps of the city square. The whole race lasts just a minute or two but thousands of people gather to watch!

In Italy, 15 August is a public holiday. There are feasts and firework displays. Many places put on horse races. The most famous one is the Palio in Siena, which is in central Italy.

FACT CAT FACT

The little village of Sedilo on Sardinia has a famous horse race each July. Hundreds of riders take part, firing their guns into the air as they gallop along.

SPORT

Football is the number one sport in Italy. Everyone supports the national team and everyone follows their local team. AC Milan and Juventus are two of the biggest clubs.

FACT CAT FACT

Italy has many places to ski. The Piedmont region around Turin in northwest Italy is on the edge of the Alps. It has more than 50 ski **resorts**.

The players on Italy's national team are known as the *Azzuri*. Find out what this nickname means.

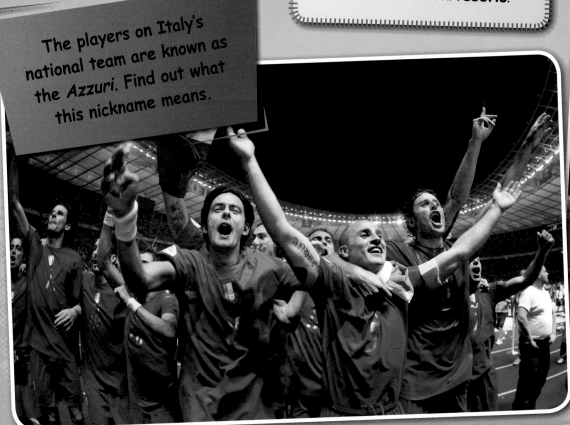

Cycling is a popular sport. Italy holds a long-distance bicycle race each year. It is called the Giro d'Italia and usually lasts 23 days.

The route of the Giro d'Italia changes each year, but the **finish line** is always in Milan.

FAMOUS PEOPLE

Two of the greatest explorers in history came from Italy.
Marco Polo was a **merchant** from Venice in the 1200s.
He is famous for his travels to Central Asia and China.
Christopher Columbus is famous
for reaching America.

Columbus first crossed
the Atlantic in 1492.
Can you find out the
name of his boat?

Maria Montessori was a doctor from Italy. She came up with new ideas about how children learn. She thought it was best for children to play, explore and find things out for themselves.

The Italians were so proud of Maria Montessori that they put her on one of their banknotes. She was on the 1,000 lire note, before Italy started using euros instead.

FACT CAT FACT

Maria Montessori's first school opened more than 100 years ago. Today, there are Montessori schools all over the world.

QUIZ

Try to answer the questions below. Look back through the book to help you. Check your answers on page 24.

1 What do people wear for the Venice Carnival?

a) sunglasses

b) fake moustaches

c) masks

2 What kind of animal is a mouflon?

a) a wild sheep

b) a wild horse

c) a wild boar

3 Cannoli from Sicily are a type of pasta. True or not true?

a) true

b) not true

4 Which city is the volcano Vesuvius near?

a) Rome

b) Naples

c) Milan

5 The Colosseum in Rome was built about 100 years ago. True or not true?

a) true

b) not true

GLOSSARY

active describes a volcano can spit out lava or ash

amphitheatre an oval or round building with rows of seats for watching shows

ancient Roman from the time, around 2,000 years ago, when Rome ruled lands in Europe, Africa and Asia

canal a manmade river

capital the city where the government (the group of people who lead a country) meets

carnival a festival where people parade in fancy dress

erupt to shoot out lava

fare the money a passenger pays for a ride

finish line the end of a race

gladiator a man trained to fight for entertainment in ancient Rome

gondola a type of flat-bottomed rowing boat used in Venice that is moved forwards with one oar

historic from long ago

landmark an important place that stands out in the landscape

lava melted rock from a volcano

mall a shopping area where there is no traffic

mammal a type of animal, often with fur, that feeds its babies milk

masked ball a party where everyone wears masks

merchant someone who travels around buying and selling things

mountain range a group of mountains – a mountain is taller, and usually more rocky, than a hill

national park an area where the landscape is protected by law so it stays wild

port a city or town with a harbour, where ships can stop and unload

ram a male sheep

rare not found or seen very often

resort a place where people go on holiday

ricotta cheese a soft Italian cheese

sea cave a cave on a coastline that has been hollowed out by the waves over a very long time

spectator someone watching something

volcano rocky hill around an opening in the Earth's surface, through which melted rock called lava can come out

INDEX

ANSWERS

Pages 4–20

page 4: The countries are San Marino in the Apennine Mountains and Vatican City, within the city of Rome.

page 6: He was Italy's first king. Italy does not have kings any more.

page 8: The three lakes are Lake Garda, Lake Maggiore and Lake Como.

page 10: The cave is called the Blue Grotto. The blue light is created by sunlight shining through seawater.

page 12: A margherita has tomato, basil and mozzarella cheese. The colours of the toppings – red, green and white – are the same colours as the Italian flag!

page 14: The last few bears live in the Abruzzo National Park. There might be as few as 30 bears left.

page 16: Carnival masks can be made of glass, china, leather or plastic.

page 18: *Azzuri* means 'the Blues'. The players all wear blue shirts.

page 20: Columbus's ship on his first voyage was the *Santa María*.

Quiz answers

1	c)	4	b)
2	a)	5	b)
3	b)		

OTHER TITLES IN THE FACT CAT SERIES...

SPACE

978 0 7502 8220 8

978 0 7502 8221 5

THE PLANETS
978 0 7502 8222 2

978 0 7502 8223 9
THE SUN

UNITED KINGDOM

978 0 7502 8433 2
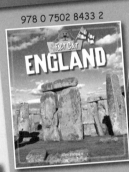
ENGLAND

NORTHERN IRELAND
978 0 7502 8440 0

978 0 7502 8439 4

SCOTLAND

WALES

978 0 7502 8438 7

HISTORY

978 0 7502 9034 0

978 0 7502 9037 1

THE WRIGHT BROTHERS
First Flight

NEIL ARMSTRONG
First Man on the Moon

978 0 7502 9040 1

978 0 7502 9031 9

CHRISTOPHER COLUMBUS
Discovering America

WAYLAND